BOOK 3

Especially for Adults

7 Late Intermediate Piano Solos for Older Students

Dennis Alexander

Over the years, my work with adult piano students has proven to be immensely rewarding and gratifying. Adults tend to be very self-motivated individuals who study piano because they love music and have always wanted to play piano, or in many cases, regret quitting piano lessons as a child. Their musical interests are different from those of children taking piano lessons. Adults need music that "warms the heart," provides opportunity for gradual technical growth and provides motivation for consistent practice.

The music in *Especially for Adults,* Book 3 is designed to accomplish all of the above. Adults will experience a real sense of accomplishment when they play these solos that contain beautiful, rich harmonies; numerous patterns that easily fit the hands and lyrical melodies that speak to their emotions. The pieces sound sophisticated and the titles themselves reflect this sophistication. In addition to the original music composed for this series, I have also arranged some favorite classical melodies that adults will know and enjoy.

The *Especially for Adults* series is the perfect supplement for any adult method book and will provide motivational repertoire in a variety of appealing styles for teenagers and adults of all ages. Enjoy!

Dennis Alexander

This series is dedicated to Lillian Livingston, my friend and musical colleague, who provided the motivation and inspiration for this project.

Cappuccino Rag

Dennis Alexander

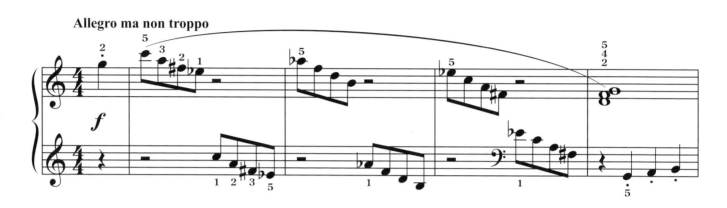

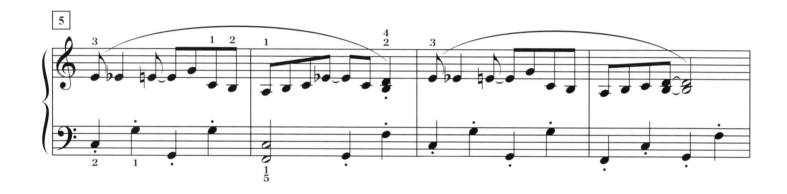

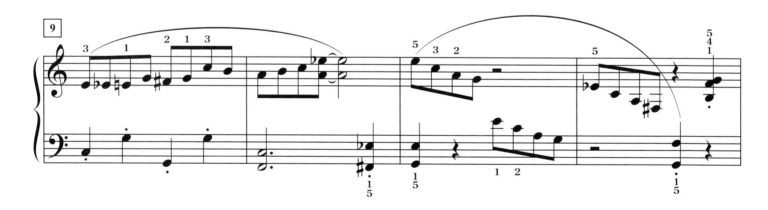

4

Nocturne in E♭ Major

Frédéric Chopin (1810–1849)
Op. 9, No. 2
Arranged by Dennis Alexander

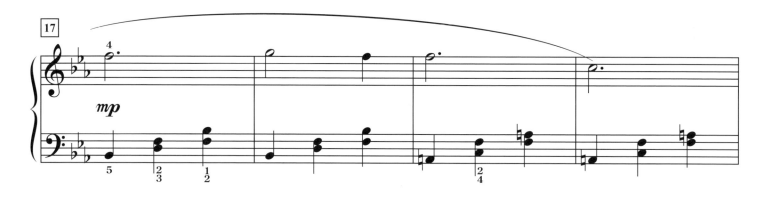

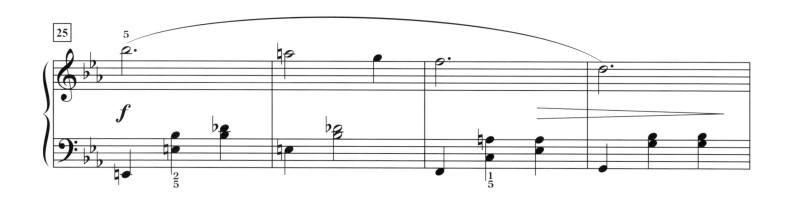

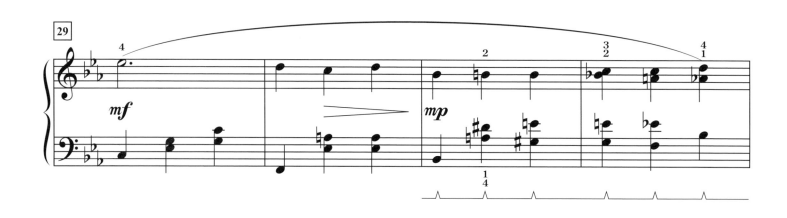

Georgetown Lake

Dennis Alexander

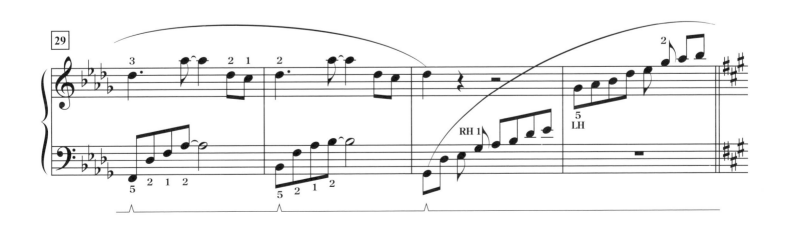

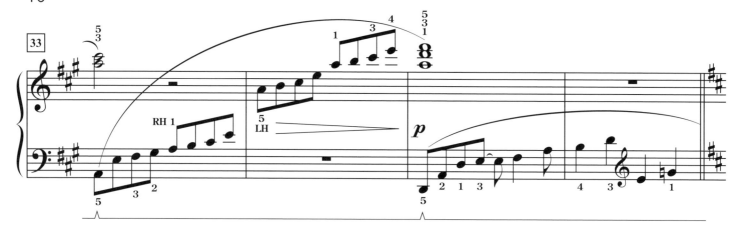

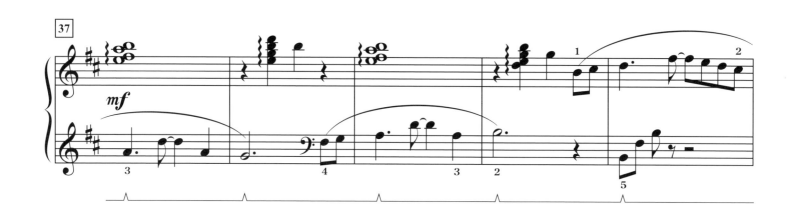

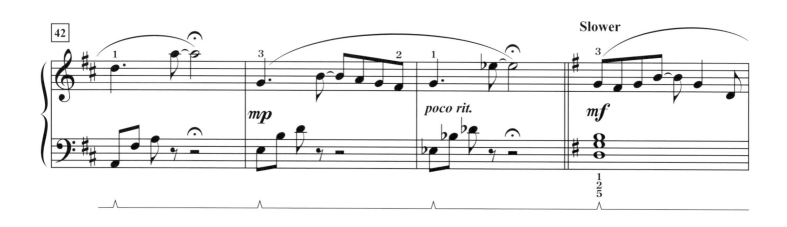

Just Groovin'

Dennis Alexander

Steady rock beat

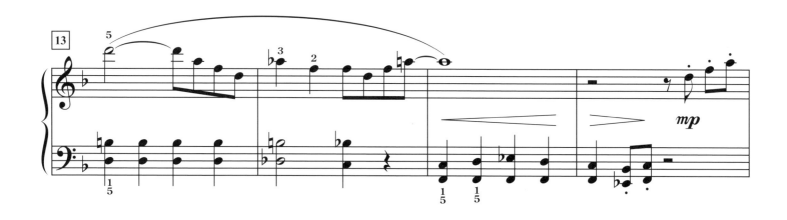

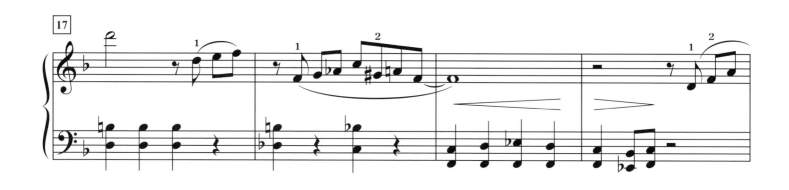

Missing You

Dennis Alexander

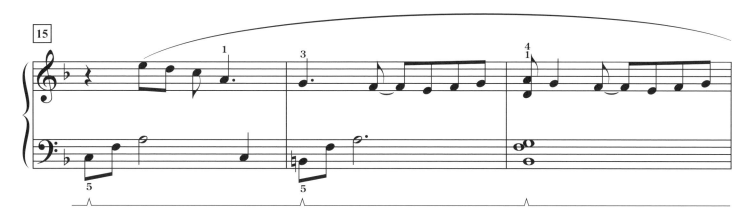

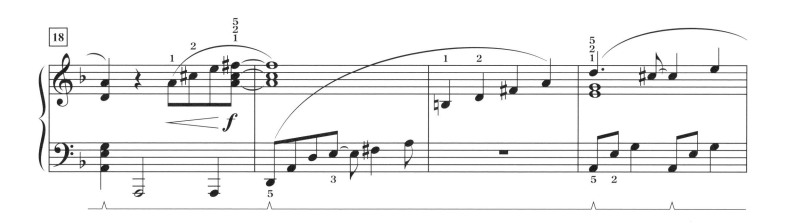

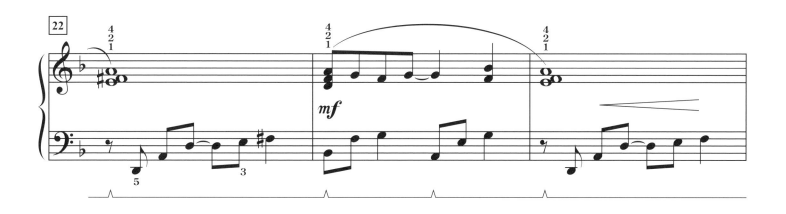

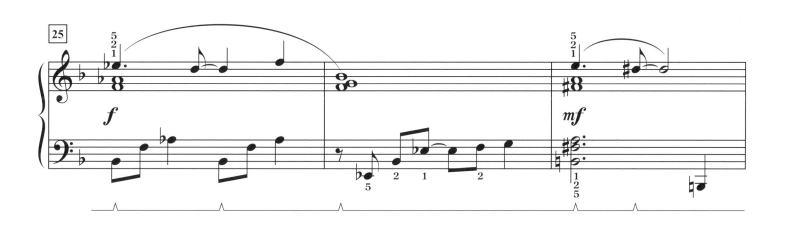

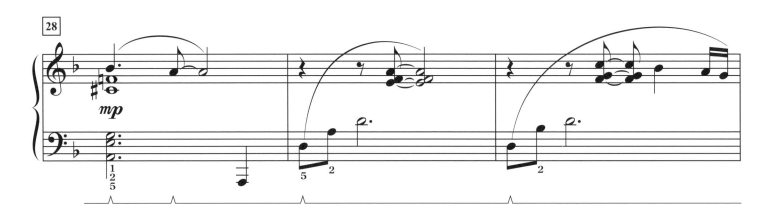

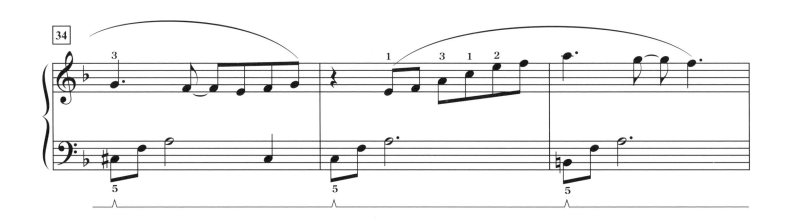

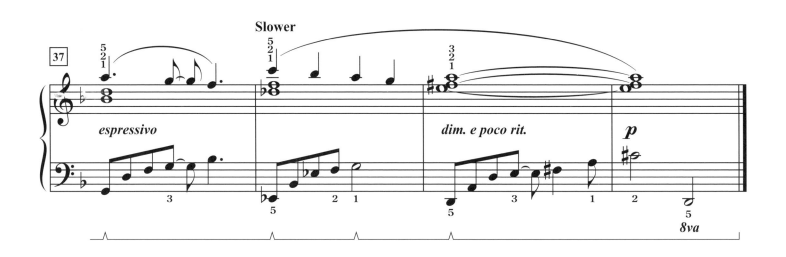

Touch a Rainbow*

Dennis Alexander

* This is an expanded version of a late-elementary piano solo by the same name (#3676)

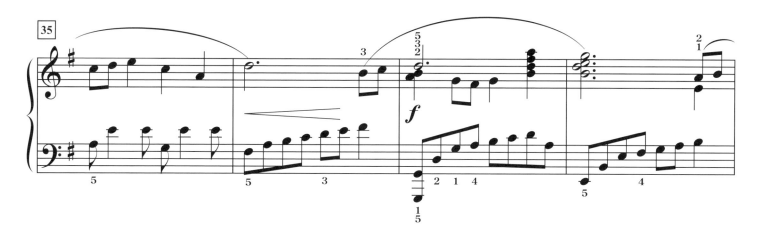

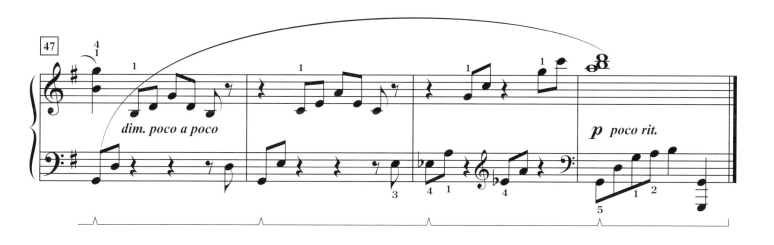

Canon in D/New World Symphony Medley

Johann Pachelbel (1653–1706)
Antonin Dvořák (1841–1904)
Arranged by Dennis Alexander

Moderato grazioso

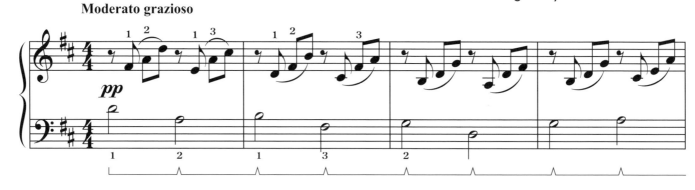

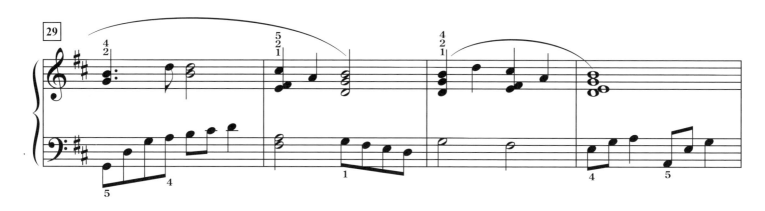

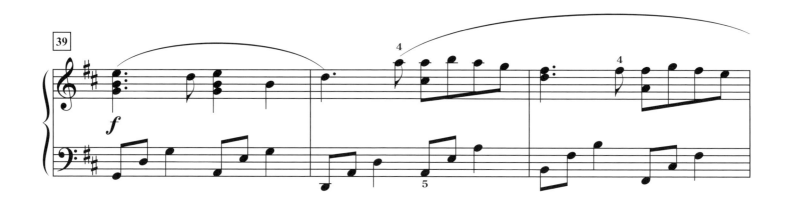

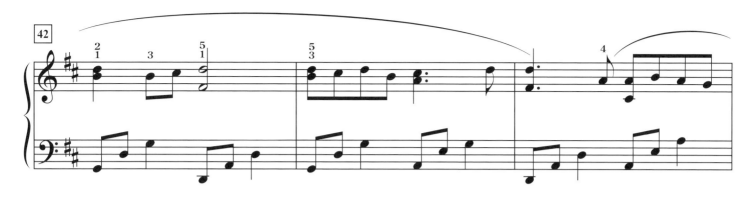

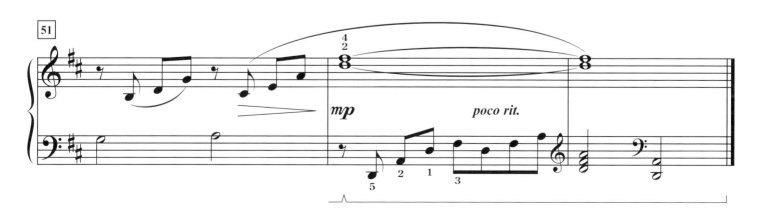